Peace for our Time?

More World War II Memories of Backwell Nailsea Tickenham and Wraxall

Author, Compiler and Editor - Peter Wright

Peter Wright

"My good friends, this is the second time in our history that there has come back from Germany to Downing Street peace with honour. I believe it is peace for our time. We thank you from the bottom of all our hearts. And now I recommend you to go home and sleep quietly in your beds".

Neville Chamberlain

Speech from the window of 10 Downing Street, 30th September 1938. Reported in The Times 1st October 1938.

"On September 2 (1939), the conflict might still have been averted - Mussolini proposed a plan for the immediate cessation of all hostilities and for peaceful megotiations. Though Germany saw her armies storming to victory, I nevertheless accepted his proposal. It was only the Franco-British war-mongers who desired war, not peace........"

Adolf Hitler

19th July 1940 Speech to the Reichstag.

A printed copy of this speech in English headed "A Last Appeal to Reason" was dropped from German planes on the night of 1/2 August 1940. (See Appendix 4 and various articles in this volume)

"There may be dark days ahead, and war can no longer be confined to the battlefield"

King George VI

3rd September 1939

"You ask what is our aim - I can answer in one word - **VICTORY!**

Winston S Churchill

13th May 1940

First published in Great Britain 1995 by Peter Wright, 5 The Perrings, Nailsea, Bristol BS19 2YD

Copyright Peter Wright and the respective contributors.

All rights reserved. No part of this publication may be reproduced, stored in a retrieval system, or transmitted in any form or by any means, electronic, mechanical, photocopying, recording, or otherwise without the prior permission of the copyright owner.

Peter Wright ISBN 0 9516257 1 3

CONTENTS
INTRODUCTION AND ACKNOWLEDGMENTS

CHAPTER ONE
WARTIME MEMORIES - RESIDENTS

BACKWELL
Never the same Again	by John Brain
The Private School at War	by Miss Barbara Lambert

NAILSEA
A Farmer's Wife	Compiled by Peter Wright *from a discussion with Ella Brake 1994*
A Doctor's Wife	by Mary Gornall
Nailsea Sub Post Office	by Muriel Chorley
Military Occupation!	Compiled by Peter Wright *from a discussion with Dora Keel in 1993*
A Plane Crash near Engine Lane	by Cecil Keel
Coombe Farm - Evacuees and the Plane Crash	Compiled by Peter Wright. *from a discussion with Jack Durbin 1994*

BACKWELL, NAILSEA AND TICKENHAM
Victory Celebrations	Compiled by Peter Wright *from a discussion with Clifford Kortright 1994*

TICKENHAM
Looking after the Evacuees	by Miss E. M. Weekes

WRAXALL
A Selection from "Wraxall in Wartime"	by Phyllis Horman
Places and People - Wraxall in the War Years	by Phyllis Horman
74th General Hospital - Christmas 1944	

CHAPTER TWO
WARTIME MEMORIES - EVACUEES

BACKWELL AND WEST TOWN
Pupils of North Hammersmith Central Mixed School.

Evacuation From London to the Country Sept 1939	by Eileen Hanlon
Late for School!	by Joan Roberts
A Happy Time!	by Grace Golding
Country Memories	by Stella Harbert

NAILSEA
Pupil of Wornington Road L.C.C. School
Evacuated to Nailsea   by Ron Howcroft

TICKENHAM
We'll Never Forget   by Gladys Wood

WRAXALL
A Selection from "Wraxall in Wartime"   by Phyllis Horman

CHAPTER THREE
AIR RAIDS

LOCAL MEMORIES   *extracts from "Villages at War"*

THE FILTON RAID, 25 SEPT, 1940,
One of their Aircraft failed to return   *from information supplied by John Perry*

The Parachutist   by Phyllis Horman

The Missing Machine Gun - A   Compiled by Peter Wright
  Mystery Solved?   *from a discussion with Don Irish*

RAIDS ON BACKWELL   compiled by Peter Wright

AIR RAID ON NAILSEA 16/17 JUNE 1941

CHAPTER FOUR
1946 THE END OR THE BEGINNING?
A Prisoner of War returns Home   by Helmuth Horst

APPENDICES

APPENDIX 1
from information supplied by Ken Wakefield
AMERICAN UNITS NEAR THIS AREA

APPENDIX 2
from information supplied by John Penny
TECHNICAL NOTES

APPENDIX 3
from information and comments (#) supplied by John Penny
GERMAN BOMBER FORCES INVOLVED IN THE RAID ON FILTON 25 SEPT 1940

APPENDIX 4
from information and comments (#) supplied by John Penny
GERMAN BOMBER FORCES INVOLVED IN THE LEAFLET RAID 1/2 AUG 1940

APPENDIX 5
from information and comments (#) supplied by John Penny
GERMAN BOMBER FORCES INVOLVED IN THE RAID 16/17 JUNE 1941

APPENDIX 6
CONTRIBUTORS, SOURCES, BIBLIOGRAPHY.

INTRODUCTION AND ACKNOWLEDGMENTS

Nearly five years ago I achieved a personal ambition by writing and publishing "Villages at War". Since then I have been seeking more information with a view to producing another book of local wartime memories.

In February 1995 I received an article by Eileen Hanlon and was spurred into action. I thought that I had almost enough information to produce a slim booklet before May 8th! But then I found so much more. This book is the result. I have drawn heavily on the experiences of others and the research of John Penny and they deserve my gratitude.

In my own research, I have not found any extensive, contemporary, personal written accounts of life in Backwell, Nailsea, Tickenham or Wraxall for the period 1939 to 1945. I expect there are many villages where there is the same lack of information.

I hope that this book, and its predecessor "Villages at War", will encourage readers to search for such items, or to write down their own memories, and to pass them onto a local archive.

In the absence of contemporaneous written accounts these recollections of momentous years may assume, in future, more importance than the writers or I intended.

I endured the early raids on London and then moved to Kent. As a result of my own experiences, and my memory of them, I find that I can easily relate to the fears and experiences of the contributors to this book.

I must finally mention the local knowledge shared with me by John Brain and Phyllis Horman without which more mistakes might have been made. Any that remain are mine alone.

I also acknowledge those who have provided me with suitable photographs to illustrate this book and the assistance that I have had from Phil Thorne and others at Adroit Printers in designing and printing this volume.

Peter Wright   Nailsea   March 1995

CHAPTER ONE

WARTIME MEMORIES - RESIDENTS

BACKWELL
NEVER THE SAME AGAIN
by John Brain

The Second World War was to change village life in Backwell for ever, even if the first year seemed to consist of relatively few real hardships. True, rationing, the blackout and the call up of men and women for active service affected every household but life continued much the same for the writer about to embark on secondary school education at Bristol Cathedral School at the age of 11 $^1/_2$.

At home my parents, with my uncle and aunt, managed West Town Bakery, with its attendant grocery and confectionery shop, and any spare time after school and every Saturday was spent helping deliver bread until late in the evening, as our rounds extended from Flax Bourton nearly into Yatton. Daily deliveries soon became restricted. "Pool" petrol as it was called became even shorter, and we could deliver to customers only on three days out of six in the working week.

Although bread was one of the few commodities not rationed, white bread was no longer allowed, and we were required to produce only the "national loaf" as it was called, a sort of half way house between a white and a wholemeal loaf with not quite the same body in it that white bread provided.

The signs of war were not long in coming. The village was flooded with evacuees from London at the outset of war, and Backwell became the home of the North Hammersmith Central School, who used different village halls as classrooms, prominent among them the large badminton hall at West Town House belonging to Mr Theodore Robinson. Luckily the nearby playing fields catered for their sporting activities. All households that had room took in evacuees, and both village and London children became friends with little trouble.

On the military side, a searchlight company was in place on the site of Backwell Comprehensive School, a gun battery was installed on Backwell Hill, and barrage balloons were constantly in position over Bristol and even more so over Avonmouth; sometimes they were lowered, but we knew when they went up the sirens would soon be signalling the approach of enemy aircraft.

Serious bombing by German planes did not really start until after the Battle of Britain; our first taste of the enemy was the dropping of propaganda leaflets over local villages: "A Last Appeal To Reason" a speech by Adolf Hitler to the German Reichstag on 19th July 1940, in which he said Britain had no chance, and should make peace. I still have a copy, as several fell in our garden.

We were at school when the first of two daylight raids on the aircraft factory at Filton caused heavy loss of life; even more dramatic for me was the string of bombs dropped in the Bristol Cathedral School yard without warning in September 1940 destroying buildings and injuring our headmaster. Only Providence saved many of us from meeting our Maker on that occasion. When night bombing started German planes flew over North Somerset on their way to bomb the Midlands and even Merseyside, and on November 24th 1940 it was Bristol's turn.

I remember to this day standing outside our back door as the city burnt - the fires turned the sky as bright as day, whilst the crash of bombs and the blasts of incessant gunfire made it a night never to be forgotten, even at my young age. That was to be the pattern of life for the next six months, as raid followed raid, and a lot of time was spent sheltering under the very table I am writing on.

We still delivered the bread throughout the blitzes; I have many memories of flares hanging in the sky over Bristol as the bombers searched for their targets; of a great clutch of incendiary bombs like so many huge sparklers dropped in the woods towards Tyntesfield, and the whistle of bombs falling now and again around our villages.

People used to come out from Bristol to avoid the raids, and one snowy night our bread van skidded to avoid a crowd walking up Plunder Street, in Cleeve, finishing up in the ditch! The garage owner at Cleeve, Mr Coward, came out in his car to tow us out whilst a raid was going on - he was a great character, and took no notice of the war in the air - we dug ourselves out of the ditch and arrived home at 12.45am!

The Good Friday raid, April 11th 1941, and the previous Friday, caused the most damage in the village at West Town, with bombs falling in much the same place on both occasions. On April 4th, three or four small bombs fell across the fields near Oldfield House, at the top of Pit Lane, the last one not so far from the road junction with Chelvey Batch. We boys were always collecting shrapnel, and I remember finding a piece of fin with a swastika and German spreadeagle on it - quite a prize! The only casualty - a horse which was in the field.

Good Friday was much worse. There was a fire decoy at Lulsgate which was lit to deceive bombers into thinking they were over Bristol. The first time this worked, but of course this meant we were in the danger area, and three quite sizeable bombs fell at the top of Charlie Gallop's yard, behind the "Rising Sun".

Damage to houses in the vicinity was extensive, mainly due to great chunks of heavy clay being blown out of the ground and crashing through the roofs of houses. At our bakery, one great wedge smashed through the roof and then the bedroom floor, finishing up in the shop below.

The sight of the village the following morning made me fear the worst, but mercifully there were no casualties, although quirks of the bomb blast put out windows in shops as far away as the old post office.

Traders cleared up the mess and carried on as usual - we were a different nation in those days, and everybody was involved. Ordinary people donned helmets and became ARP wardens, firefighters, members of the Home Guard, in addition to their own work.

Workers at Mr Osmond's Engineering factory in West Town *John Brain*

There was quite a large war factory run by Mr A.W. Osmond, an engineer, situated behind the old butcher's shop at West Town, now occupied by Mrs Figg at 61 West Town Road. The workforce, mainly female, totalled around 60, most of whom

A LAST APPEAL TO REASON

BY

ADOLF HITLER

Speech before the Reichstag, 19th July, 1940

I have summoned you to this meeting in the midst of our tremendous struggle for the freedom and the future of the German nation. I have done so, firstly, because I considered it imperative to give our own people an insight into the events, unique in history, that lie behind us, secondly, because I wished to express my gratitude to our magnificent soldiers, and thirdly, with the intention of appealing, once more and for the last time, to common sense in general.

If we compare the causes which prompted this historic struggle with the magnitude and the far-reaching effects of military events, we are forced to the conclusion that its general course and the sacrifices it has entailed are out of all proportion to the alleged reasons for its outbreak — unless they were nothing but a pretext for underlying intentions.

The programme of the National-Socialist Movement, in so far as it affected the future development of the Reich's relations with the rest of the world, was simply an attempt to bring about a definite revision of the Treaty of Versailles, though as far as at all possible, this was to be accomplished by peaceful means.

This revision was absolutely essential. The conditions imposed at Versailles were intolerable, not only because of their humiliating discrimination and because the disarmament which they ensured deprived the German nation of all its rights, but far more so because of the consequent destruction of the material existence of one of the great civilized nations in the world, and the proposed annihilation of its future, the utterly senseless accumulation of immense tracts of territory under the domination of a number of States, the theft of all the irreparable foundations of life and indispensable vital necessities from a conquered nation. While this dictate was being drawn up, men of insight even among our foes were uttering warnings about the terrible consequences which the ruthless application of its insane conditions would entail — a proof that even among them the conviction predominated that such a dictate could not possibly be upheld in days to come. Their objections and protests were silenced by the assurance that the statutes of the newly-created League of Nations provided for a revision of these conditions; in fact, the League was supposed to be the competent authority. The hope of revision was thus at no time regarded as presumptuous, but as something natural. Unfortunately, the Geneva institution, as those responsible for Versailles had intended, never looked upon itself as a body competent to undertake any sensible revision, but from the very outset as nothing more than the guarantor of the ruthless enforcement and maintenance of the conditions imposed at Versailles.

All attempts made by democratic Germany to obtain equality for the German people by a revision of the Treaty proved unavailing.

World War Enemies Unscrupulous Victors

It is always in the interests of a conqueror to represent stipulations that are to his advantage as sacrosanct, while the instinct of self-preservation in the vanquished leads him to reacquire the common human rights that he has lost. For him the dictate of an overbearing conqueror had all the less legal force, since he had never been honourably conquered. Owing to a rare misfortune, the German Empire, between 1914 and 1918, lacked good leadership. To this, and to the as yet unenlightened faith and trust placed by the German people in the words of democratic statesmen, our downfall was due.

Hence the Franco-British claim that the Dictate of Versailles was a sort of international, or even a supreme, code of laws, appeared to be nothing more than a piece of insolent arrogance to every honest German, the assumption, however, that British or French statesmen should actually claim to be the guardians of justice, and even of human culture, as mere stupid effrontery. A piece of effrontery that is thrown into a sufficiently glaring light by their own extremely negligible achievements in this direction. For seldom have any countries in the world been ruled with a lesser degree of wisdom, morality and culture than those which are at the moment exposed to the ragings of certain democratic statesmen.

The programme of the National-Socialist Movement, besides freeing the Reich from the innermost fetters of a small substratum of Jewish-capitalistic and pluto-democratic profiteers, proclaimed to the world our resolution to shake off the shackles of the Versailles Dictate.

Germany's demands for this revision were a vital necessity and essential to the existence and honour of every great nation. They will probably one day be regarded by posterity as extremely reasonable. In practice, all these demands had to be carried through contrary to the will of the Franco-British rulers. We all regarded it as a sure sign of successful leadership in the Third Reich that for years we were able to effect this revision without a war. Not that — as the British and French demagogues asserted — we were at that time incapable of fighting. When, thanks to growing common sense, it finally appeared as though international co-operation might lead to a peaceful solution of the remaining problems, the Agreement to this end signed in Munich on September 29, 1938, by the four leading interested States, was not only not welcomed in London and Paris, but was actually condemned as a sign of abominable weakness. Now that peaceful revision threatened to be crowned with success, the Jewish capitalist war-mongers, their hands stained with blood, saw their tangible pretexts for realizing their diabolical plans vanish into thin air. Once again we witnessed a conspiracy by wretched corruptible political creatures and money-grabbing financial magnates, for whom war was a welcome means of furthering their business ends. The poison scattered by the Jews throughout the nations began to exercise its disintegrating influence on sound common sense. Scribblers concentrated upon decrying honest men, who wanted peace, as weaklings and traitors, and upon denouncing the opposition parties as the Fifth Column, thus breaking all internal resistance to their criminal war policy. Jews and Freemasons, armaments manufacturers and war profiteers, international business-men and Stock Exchange jobbers seized upon political hirelings of the desperado and Herostrates type, who described war as something infinitely desirable.

It was the work of these criminal persons that spurred the Polish State on to adopt an attitude that was out of all proportion to Germany's demands and still less to the attendant consequences.

In its dealings with Poland, the German Reich has pre-eminently exercised genuine self-restraint since the National-Socialist régime came into power. One of the most despicable and foolish measures of the Versailles Dictate, namely, the severance of an old German province from the Reich, was crying out aloud for revision. Yet what were my requests?

I name myself in this connexion, because no other statesman might have dared to propose a solution such as mine to the German nation. It merely implied the return of Danzig — an ancient purely German city — to the Reich, and the creation of a means of communication between the Reich and its severed province. Even this was to be decided by a plebiscite subject to the control of an international body. If Mr Churchill and the rest of the war-mongers had felt a fraction of the responsibility towards Europe which inspired me, they could never have begun their infamous game.

It was only due to these and other European and non-European parties and their war interests, that Poland rejected my proposals, which in no way affected either her honour or her existence, and in their stead had recourse to terror and to the sword. In this case we once more showed unexampled and truly superhuman self-control, since for months, despite murderous attacks on minority Germans, and even despite the slaughter of tens of thousands of our German fellow-countrymen, we still sought an understanding by peaceful means.

What was the situation?

One of the most unnatural creations of the Dictate of Versailles, a popinjay puffed up with political and military pomp, insults another State for months on end and threatens to grind it to powder, to fight battles on the outskirts of Berlin, to hack the German armies to pieces, to extend its frontiers to the Oder or the Elbe, and so forth. Meanwhile, the other State, Germany, watches this tumult in patient silence, although a single movement of her arm would have sufficed to prick this bubble inflated with folly and hatred.

On September 2, the conflict might still have been averted — Mussolini proposed a plan for the immediate cessation of all hostilities and for peaceful negotiations. Though Germany saw her armies storming to victory, I nevertheless accepted his proposal. It was only the Franco-British war-mongers who desired war, not peace. More than that, as Mr Chamberlain said, they needed a long war, because they had now invested their capital in armaments shares, had purchased machinery and required time for the development of their business interests and the amortisation of their investments. For, after all, what do these "citizens of the world" care about Poles, Czechs or such-like peoples?

On June 19, 1940, a German soldier found a curious document when searching some railway trucks standing in the station of La Charité. As the document bore a distinctive inscription, he immediately handed it over to his commanding officer. It was then passed on to other quarters, where it was soon realized that we had lighted on an important discovery. The station was subjected to another, more thorough-going search.

Thus it was that the German High Command gained possession of a collection of documents of unique historical significance. They were the secret documents of the Allied Supreme War Council, and included the minutes of every meeting held by this illustrious body. This time Mr. Churchill will not succeed in contesting or lying about the veracity of these documents, as he tried to do when documents were discovered in Warsaw.

These documents bear marginal notes inscribed by Messieurs Gamelin, Daladier, Weygand, etc. They can therefore at any time be confirmed or refuted by these very gentlemen. They further yield remarkable evidence of the machinations of the war-mongers and war-extenders. Above all, they show that those stony-hearted politicians regarded all the small nations as a means to their ends; that they had attempted to use Finland in their own interests; that they had determined to turn Norway and Sweden into a theatre of war; that they had planned to fan a conflagration in the Balkans in order to gain the assistance of a hundred divisions from those countries; that they had planned a bombardment of Batum and Baku by a ruthless and unscrupulous interpretation of Turkey's neutrality, who was not unfavourable to them; that they had inveigled Belgium and the Netherlands more and more completely, until they finally entrapped them into binding General Staff agreements, and so on, ad libitum.

The documents further give a picture of the dilettante methods by which these political war-mongers tried to quench the blaze which they had lighted, of their democratic militarism, which is in part to blame for the appalling fate that they have inflicted on hundreds of thousands, even millions of their own soldiers, of their barbarous unscrupulousness which caused them callously to force mass evacuation on their peoples, which brought them no military advantages, though the effects on the population were outrageously cruel.

These same criminals are responsible for having driven Poland into war.

Eighteen days later this campaign was, to all intents and purposes, at an end.

Britain and France Considered Understanding a Crime

On October 6, 1939, I addressed the German nation for the second time during this war at this very place. I was able to inform them of our glorious military victory over the Polish State. At the same time I appealed to the insight of the responsible men in the enemy States and to the nations themselves. I warned them not to continue this war, the consequences of which could only be devastating. I particularly warned the French of embarking on a war which would forcibly eat its way across the frontier and which, irrespective of its outcome, would have appalling consequences. At the same time, I addressed this appeal to the rest of the world, although I feared — as I expressly said — that my words would not be heard, but would more than ever arouse the fury of the interested war-mongers. Everything happened as I predicted. The responsible elements in Britain and France scented in my appeal a dangerous attack on their war profits. They therefore immediately began to declare that every thought of conciliation was out of the question, nay, even a crime; that the war had to be pursued in the name of civilization, of humanity, of happiness, of progress, and — to leave no stone unturned — in the name of religion itself. For this purpose, negroes and bushmen were to be mobilized. Victory, they then said, would come of its own accord, it was, in fact, within their easy reach, as I myself must know very well and have known for a long time since, or I should not have broadcast my appeal for peace throughout the world. For if I had had any justification for were local people. Mr Osmond's main business was in Hotwells, and I sometimes was given a lift to school, as his two boys also went to the Cathedral School. Lessons were never cancelled due to the blitzes, and somehow we carried on our education, despite the constant dislocation of dashing off to the air raid shelters when the sirens sounded.

On some half days, when sports were cancelled I used to visit a schoolboy friend, Bill Shewan, whose family lived just in front of the old glassworks in Nailsea, where we spent many happy hours, or else went to look at the bomb craters in the fields around. One day we even poked around amongst a pile of what we were told were anti personnel mines dumped up on Cadbury Camp for safety!

So many more memories come back. The big American camp at Brockley where we used to scrounge cigarettes (!); the Oxford training plane from Lulsgate which came down on the road leading up to Chelvey Batch killing both crew members; the big village occasions like "Salute the Soldier" week, a bit like Backwell's Festival weeks of recent times, when local events were arranged and the money raised given to National Savings for the war effort.

And finally the VE day celebrations themselves, with a church service "many people standing in the aisles and others unable to gain admission" as the parish magazine reported.

A bonfire on the hill that night, an impromptu tea for the children and a social gathering at the parish hall the next day brought down the curtain on those five momentous years. Three months later the Japanese were to be defeated and we would be at peace, but all our lives had been changed, and the quiet life of pre-war Backwell was gone for ever.

THE PRIVATE SCHOOL AT WAR
by Miss Barbara Lambert

It seemed as if the school would not be able to continue. People were planning to take away their children to safer areas. Mrs Cave and Mrs Harrington Fry called a meeting of parents, and a few guaranteed that they would leave their children with me if I would carry on.

Miss Barbara Lambert with her first pupils in 1936
Fairfield PNEU School Archive

The next trouble was that it seemed likely that the building would be taken from me to house the evacuees who were arriving in Backwell from London. However, things gradually settled down and we started the term on September 20th with 7 out of the 17 children of the previous term. Gradually the children came back and other children came from dangerous areas to live in the surrounding district. The parents contributed to a fund and we had a blast wall built outside the school door. This never had to deal with a blast but it certainly helped to keep out the draught *(it was still there in 1965.)*.

There is not time to tell you of all the difficulties of war-time school, but as the numbers increased we had to find some means of keeping the children at school all day, and giving them lunch. At first we went to a small cafe that used to be on the main road. Then for a while we lunched at the

George Inn, and finally the children had to bring their own pack lunch. (It is interesting to note that at that time you could not buy a thermos flask without a doctor's certificate).

We all felt that this was not a good arrangement for small children so we made a plan that every week each mother should send something from her family's rationed food. Also they all brought a set of cutlery and two plates - this added interest to the lunches in wondering whose knife you were using, or who owned a certain plate. My sister came to cook the lunches for me.

By this time I had taken a furnished house in Farleigh near the school called "Fairfield", and here we were used to go daily for our lunch. All went well for a couple of months, then we discovered that it was illegal to use personal rations in this way - which was a pity as it had seemed such an excellent solution to our problems. As it was a private school we were unable to obtain the school meals as supplied to the State schools so we applied for, and finally were given, a catering License. After a while my sister had to give up the lunches due to her family ties, so Miss Fayle came along in February 1945.

(From an article previously published in Pennant by permission of Mrs Nosowska Headteacher Fairfield PNEU School)

NAILSEA
A FARMER'S WIFE
by Peter Wright
from a discussion with Ella Brake 1994

Ella told me when the evacuees arrived I was one of the people who had to deliver them to their billets. I took 4 children to a lovely house where children were almost unknown. Several weeks later I was accosted by the woman who lived there and was accused of introducing measles to the establishment.

We took in a young postman's wife with a baby but she returned to London a few months later. Eventually we had four private evacuees from Bristol for several years. They were charged a total of £2 per week and for this they were supplied with food and coal and two rooms.

I helped at Mrs Cowlin's "British Restaurant" once or twice a week. Mrs Cowlin lived at the Elms. *(Editor's note - Subsequently found to be built on the site of "Middle Engine Pit" the remains of which are to be preserved)* Mrs Cowlin was inclined to be concerned about the American men's attitude to the ladies.

From the high ground on which Battens farm stands there is a good view to the west. I saw a large number of aircraft on one occasion and said to Kathy my help "My goodness they are Jerries". Kathy rushed upstairs to gather my youngest daughter and we all went into the shelter where, to keep our minds occupied, we cut up enough carrots for a week.

Kathy used to go to Nailsea Court to "Knit for the Forces".

On one occasion I was at my mother-in-laws when a raid started on Bristol. I knew that I had to get home as my husband, being a special constable, would probably be called out. As I cycled towards the farm I thought that he had all the lights on. It turned out to be the light of the fires in Bristol. Bright enough to read a paper.

A DOCTOR'S WIFE
by Mary Gornall

So Britain was at war! It seemed impossible to believe. The golden autumn days continued, but everything else was suddenly in chaos.

I was 8 months pregnant with our first child and had 4 London boys and a teacher to look after. Fortunately they were clean and reasonably well behaved; no thanks to the master for this; he was romantically involved with a female teacher and we seldom saw him.

After the first few days there was not an apple left on a tree in Nailsea. One of our boys, asked to do a small job, informed me gloomily that he had a "bad heart"; all the same he was first in the queue to swing out from the arm of Harry Wyatt's windmill.

We had the children at home for half of each school day, as they had alternate sessions with the local children to begin with. Soon head-lice were a problem with the whole junior population, hosts as well as guests, and our surgery was the de-nitting centre on 2 or 3 afternoons each week. The District Nurses had local volunteers (including huge me) to assist them, and I can recall the awful smell of the oil that was used whenever I remember that time.

After a few weeks our evacuees were found other homes in the village; some kindly souls had offered accommodation but had not had any assigned to them.

Dr White had volunteered for the R.A.M.C. and was called up on day 8; from then on my husband, Arthur Gornall, was left to run the hugely swollen practice on his own. Besides Nailsea Tickenham Wraxall and parts of Failand, Flax Bourton and Backwell were all in his care. I seemed to be permanently answering the phone, revising visiting lists, cleaning up the surgery and waiting room and washing bottles.

We did all the dispensing for "private" patients, and Fred Webster made up all the prescriptions for "panel" patients.

(NB for those too young to remember life before the National Health Service "panel" patients were those in paid work, usually male; "private" patients who paid the doctor for treatment were the wives, children, retired people; some of the latter belonged to Friendly Clubs, Oddfellows etc which meant a mine strewn field for book keeping!)

We had some short spells of assistance in the practice; my sister was one and she was very popular. There was a retired doctor living in Cleeve and a lady doctor bombed out of Birmingham who was staying with her mother. These offered a little help during the worst months of January to March but mostly we had to cope alone. In 1944 we heard of Dr Willoughby who had been forced to leave missionary work in China and he joined us permanently becoming a great friend to everyone.

Nailsea had some splendid District Nurses; Lily Welsher, Molly and Bridie Cummins who together with Nurse Hynam in Wraxall / Flax Bourton and Nurse Weekes in Backwell and Nurse Jones in Long Ashton were of enormous support. At that time it was usual for babies to be born at home; hospital deliveries were for "difficult" cases. In wartime, with petrol severely rationed and the hazards of travelling along unlit winding lanes with the feeble cowled lamps we were forced to use, attendance at hospital was something to be avoided if possible. These dedicated women were out and about on their bikes at all hours of the day and night in all weathers with seldom a day off. Yet they never grumbled nor flagged in their skilled attention to all sections of the community.

In our house we were almost always entertaining visitors, sometimes on floors as well as in beds. There were relatives and 'Bristol' friends whose homes had been damaged; parents of evacuee children and of sons in the Naval Convalescent Unit at Barrow Gurney; and American medical inspectors visiting the Tyntesfield Hospital.

Parents visiting evacuees in Nailsea
Janet Saunders

I had morning help from friends in the neighbourhood: Muriel Flook, Doreen Caple, Edith Gould, Doris Griffin, Mrs Sullivan. At different times, singly, or in pairs, they would help me with the house and children as I seemed to be permanently on the phone every morning.

My mother and both sisters were very good and came on occasional afternoons so that I could do some shopping in Bristol and at the same time stock up the dispensary shelves. Twice I was caught up in air raids while on these expeditions, which was not pleasant at all. Once I fondly imagined my family to be safe while I was in danger but when I got home I found the bombs had been very close indeed to our house. Next time it was the other way round and I was the one who had to go a long way home through Whitchurch to avoid the rubble strewn streets.

Before the war we had started to make a garden out of the field in which our house was built. Now we were commanded to "Dig for Victory". So our part-time gardener Charlie Gray, with a great deal of help from Arthur Lasson and Tom Atkins, as lads of all work, kept us provided with vegetables and fruit for ourselves with some to share. How they performed such a miracle from our rough ground was a mystery, but their splendid efforts were appreciated by many besides ourselves.

In 1941 the grandly named "British Restaurant" opened in the Brotherhood Hall (now Toc H) and served lunches for 2/- (10p) on 3 or 4 days a week. Mrs Cowlin was the moving spirit in getting it all started and she was responsible to the Ministry of Food for the purchase of supplies and for the accounts. Her assistants included Ida Tuckey, Ella Brake, Irene Pinneger, and many others but these were my colleagues when I became a "Tuesday - kitchen - maid". We cooked stew mainly (lots of gravy!), with two vegetables and a boiled suet pudding (we all got scalded and evaded the cloth washing whenever we could) or rice and jam.

This substantial meal, washed down with cups of tea, was excellent value for money. It proved a boon to harassed housewives and to those living alone, for whom the meagre rations were a great trial. We were very fortunate as patients were very generous. A farmer's wife would press Arthur to take a pat of butter "for the children", a beekeeper gave us honey, one patient regularly fished in Blagdon Lake, another was a crack shot at rabbits and pheasants. We had a large garden which we had turned over from flowers to vegetables and fruit.

We also kept hens, so we were able to share our produce with the needy or convalescent. One wonderful day a young sailor brought us a banana, something we had not seen for years. We had a fun ceremony, cutting it into 8 pieces on our largest carving-dish, but Peter (aged 4) thought it was horrid and spat out his bit at once!

As time wore on the monotony of life meant that many people were feeling quite poorly and under strain. Recreation and sport were almost non-existent. The radio kept us informed and amused with news 3 or 4 times a day. Then there was 'Housewives Choice', or 'Workers Playtime', broadcasts to the Forces, Children's Hour (it was a whole hour too) beside the serial plays, 'ITMA' or 'Bandwagon' to look forward to. Churchill made regular stirring broadcasts denouncing the "Naaazees" and Herr Hitler in his deep rolling growl, and we took heart from them. There was also a great feeling of community and a readiness to give help that is hard to describe in this time of plenty and of dependence on Social Services.

Neighbours really were good neighbours; they ran errands, did shopping, sat up with the lonely or frightened, braved the inky dark and the bombers overhead to reach a phone and summon the doctor. Bill Harvill carried pick-a-back an injured child from the West End to the surgery for stitching. A woman who fell and injured her back was laid out flat on Arthur Wyatt's coal lorry that had just made a delivery nearby. Everyone had tales to tell about how good their neighbours were.

And then, at last, it was all over!

With the bells ringing again it seemed as if the whole population was out on the village green or the High Street. Certainly the waiting room was nearly empty; so, leaving the boys tucked up in bed with Arthur to watch both of them and to listen for the phone I joined the crowd, singing, laughing, weeping and holding hands.

Victory Party *Cis Weeks*

Outside the Royal Oak an impromptu dance was going on and I had my whirl with Jack Willoughby and another inhabitant or two as well as a brace of American hospital orderlies still in their khaki ward-coats. Then I went home and Arthur joined the crowd; he said it was the only night in 6 years that he refused to discuss any ailment with anybody!

I think we had our supper about midnight and began to calm down a little. The days to come would be hard, we knew - and they were - but on that magical May night we were sure we could survive them as well.

(Editor's Note - Mrs Gornall later taught at the Fairfield School the wartime story of which has been briefly related above by Miss Barbara Lambert in "The Private School at War".)

NAILSEA SUB POST OFFICE
by Muriel Chorley

My parents took over the Nailsea sub Post office on 31st August 1939 and were there until 1952 so they saw the village through the war. I lived there until 1943 when I joined the W.R.N.S. but I have several memories of the early days of the war.

The bomb which fell on 31st May 1941 killing a cow did damage to the Congregational Church. In those days it was a small chapel reached along a dark and often muddy path.

The huge lumps of clay thrown up by the bomb crashed all over the place; one piece crashing against the front door of the Post office. Luckily the door withstood the shock as it had been reinforced with iron in the times when coal mining was being carried on and drunken miners passed by.

I was sleeping on a mattress on the floor and quite thought my last hour had come. I still remember hearing the bomb whistling as it came down.

MILITARY OCCUPATION!
*Compiled by Peter Wright
from a discussion with Dora Keel in 1993*

(Mrs Keel and her husband ran the Butchers Arms during the war)

During the war the Army requisitioned a room and the skittle alley and Dora and her husband had three sergeants and a Sergeant Major Locke of the R.A.S.C. staying there. They were attached to the troops at the Masonic Hall. She went on to say:

On one occasion my daughter Doreen and I saw four armed soldiers coming with one in the middle. They marched up stairs and we wondered what was happening so we went upstairs and knelt down and listened and heard someone say "28 days in the Glasshouse".

We hurriedly went downstairs and said to the sergeant what we had heard. He said that the prisoner would have to go to Shepton Mallet. The Sergeant Major was unable to get the prisoner in and phoned around without success so he asked me whether I knew of an empty house or cottage.

I recommended one near to the Comrades Club and told him that he could get the key from Long Ashton.

He obtained the key and put the prisoner there with two guards. Before this the prisoner had been kept in the skittle alley. The two guards used the pub and the customers could not see why the prisoner should be deprived and arrangements were made to send him a drink.

After a while another prisoner arrived. I believe the first may have hit an officer at Portishead. They were kept busy scrubbing the clubroom and emptying the bucket toilets that we then had.

At Christmas (probably 1939) the sergeant major wanted to go home but could not leave the prisoners. I talked it over with one or two people who lived in Ridgeway and two of them offered to take the prisoners into their homes. So off went the sergeant major to Macclesfield? and the two prisoners had to promise to return on a certain day.

I remember the Filton Raid. We had cookery classes there that day (as we had done for some time as the school was not large enough to cope). The cookery teacher had the children in the passageway and we watched the German aircraft from the doorstep. They were all spread out.

(Her son Cecil was at Yatton that day and remembers seeing a Spitfire attack the German planes. He also remembers a bomb dropping one evening in Watery Lane.)

A PLANE CRASH NEAR ENGINE LANE by Cecil Keel

"Came from the direction of Wraxall ... caught the lower cable .... awful mess ... one body in the hedge ... " (VAW)

Airspeed Oxford,
Official silhouette used during the war

When I was about 15 I was going down on the Moor to go shooting when an aeroplane hit the high tension wires and crashed near Engine Lane killing all on board. I believe a couple may have still been alive when I got there. Dr Gornall came to the scene.

Editor's Note - This was an Airspeed Oxford from 286 Sqdn RAF Locking which crashed on 17th December 1942 killing the pilot Sgt Hammond and 2 others.

(Details from "Somerset at War" by Mac Hawkins pub by The Dovecote Press. Other recollections of this crash appear in "Villages at War" and the article below).

COOMBE FARM - EVACUEES AND THE PLANE CRASH IN DECEMBER 1942

Compiled by Peter Wright from a discussion with Jack Durbin 1994

Jack and his wife had three lots of evacuees staying at the farm. They came from Hammersmith and Kensington. The last family, the Hollelys stayed for some time after hostilities had ended. He told me:

I remember that one of the children with the first group of evacuees, a seven year old by the name of Lennie, started to go around the farm jumping on the ducklings. I had to stop this and told his mother. I felt rather sorry for her as she had come away from the risks of staying in London and now found her son in my bad books.

(On 17th December 1942) We were having our tea when Gwen came rushing in and said "A plane has crashed". We didn't really believe her. She had to get quite angry to get us moving. She had seen the flash as it hit the wires. It was about 4 fields from Engine Lane. The crash site, when we found it, was in a field belonging to William Hobbs farm (not to our farm as previous accounts seem to indicate).

Royston Hobbs' dad and I were the first there. I ran back to the farm to call the Doctor. One poor chap was wrapped round the tree and although there were movements in the bodies I am sure that they were dead and had been killed instantly. We discovered that the plane (an Airspeed Oxford) had been flying from Filton To Weston Super Mare).

BACKWELL, NAILSEA AND TICKENHAM
VICTORY CELEBRATIONS

Compiled by Peter Wright from a discussion with Clifford Kortright 1994

For much of the war the ringing of church bells was banned, as they were reserved to warn of an invasion. The ban had been lift-

Victory Party Chapel Alley
Jack Clement

ed well before June 10th 1944 when we rang a full peal to celebrate E.J. "Ted" Baker's 50 years as a ringer.

On VE day we started to ring at 6am and continued for much of the day with occasional breaks. There was only one day's public holiday at that time but for Victory over Japan in August we had three.

I remember going to one celebration, outside the New Inn at West End, followed by another, at Grove Farm Backwell with the Vowles family, and a third at Tickenham where I also had friends. This must have been in August 1945 as I could not have done this all in one day.

TICKENHAM
LOOKING AFTER THE EVACUEES
by Miss E. M. Weekes

First of all came the evacuees, two sisters, Margaret and Gladys Hodgson from Barking Essex. They stayed with us until 23 June 1945. I believe that they were the last to go home from the villages around us. In fact both of them went to work in Clevedon, Margaret went to Sibleys (grocer) in Hill Road and Gladys also worked in a shop in the same road.

The girls had their bikes sent from home and we took them all around the villages when it was quiet enough to do so, the first months of the war were quiet and one day we took them shopping in Bristol. Whilst we were there the sirens went and I suppose it made Margaret think (she had just turned 12 years). She said to Mr Durbin

"Pa? If anything happens to our Mum and Dad will you keep us for all time?"

In time all their family came for weekends father, mother, gran, their twin sisters and their husbands, they were only too pleased to have a quiet weekend after the noise of London.

When the war started we had to get whatever we could to make blackout curtains and the windows had white material about 2 inches wide stuck on to make squares. The idea of this was to stop any glass from flying about should there be any bomb blast. We were fortunate and did not experience any bombs very near us.

We were all issued with gas masks and identity cards which we were told to carry with us at all times wherever we went. I must not forget the ration cards, without these we could not get any food most of which was in short supply. If we went anywhere we made sure we were home before blackout time as we did not have to show any cycle or torch lights. Once the guns and searchlights started and the planes came over it ceased to be quiet. We had friends in Bristol who were bombed out so they had our bedrooms and we (five of us) slept in the passage for a time. Then the folks bought an Anderson shelter, a galvanised affair which we let into the ground and covered with soil and shrubs. We went down steps to it and had makeshift bunk beds; we felt a bit safer at night. I remember coming out one morning very early after the all clear sounded. It had been a very noisy night and to my surprise the nightingales were singing one over the other. It was lovely to hear them after the guns.

Another morning we could hear a bell ringing and thought that the Germans had landed somewhere (as we understood that the church bells would ring if they did land) however the ringing turned out to be a bell buoy in Walton Bay over the hill from us. At the end of Court Lane Clevedon there was a stone shed and this had holes around its walls so that guns could be fired should the enemy have come.

Our air raid warden was "Joe Haskins" a market gardener who lived near us. There were two brothers working in their market garden when the planes came over that did so much damage at Filton aerodrome. As the brothers realised that they were German planes they took to their heels, jumped our garden gate to try to get some shelter as by this time guns all around were firing at the aircraft. These planes took us all by surprise.

By this time we were wondering how many more people we could put up in our beds. We had our friends from Bristol, then a couple came from Clifton, finally a lady and her little girl came from London when the doodlebugs came over. Her husband came for weekends. I think I am right when I say there was a searchlight and I believe a gun at Mr Court's farm at Nailsea West End and search lights at Lower Failand.

We had a German prisoner of war camp at Sixty Acres, Failand and somehow three of them got to know that my father was ill in bed. They came to see if they could sit with him and one of them came regularly. He was a barber and he used to cut father's hair and shave him and would sit at his bedside until it was time to go back to camp. Three of them were at Father's funeral. They were not all bad, but had to fight the same as our own men did whether they wanted to or not.

Some of those days were not without their humourous side; for instance one night it became very noisy so off we went to the shelter. One person was missing; an elderly lady relative. We went back indoors to hurry her up and, would you believe it, she insisted on using a torch so that she could see to put her hair tidy. When we finally got her away from the mirror she said "Blast and seize old Hitler I wish the old fellow (meaning the devil) had him".

On another occasion I was at my parents' home at Failand. As tea was in short supply I used to take a spoonful with me so that I could have a cup before returning to Tickenham. However this time it was not tea in the packet, but some special onion seed for my brother.

Mother made me a cup of tea! That was the end of the onion seed!

The time came when our evacuees belongings were collected by the railway van and taken to Clevedon and off they went. It was like losing sisters when they went home. They soon came back with their boy friends for holidays. It was a lot of work at the time but we had some happy times.

The years roll on and I am still in touch with Margaret and Gladys. Both of them are now grandmothers and the eldest a widow; they will, I hope, be writing their own memories.

(Editor - see Chapter 2)

(From an article previously published in Pennant)

WRAXALL

A SELECTION FROM "WRAXALL IN WARTIME"
by Phyllis Horman

Dad built an air - raid shelter and when the warning sounded we, and the lady and her daughter next door all trooped into it. It was very comfortable, really, but later on we had a problem. There were many springs in Wraxall and one or two of them were in the Grove, one being near our shelter. We must have had an extra amount of rain one winter or spring and the water came in or up.

Everything was taken out of the shelter to dry, but I made good use of the water. Our only means of having a bath was to use a galvanised one in front of the fire. These baths were also used for the weekly wash and they hung on the wall near the back door when not in use. The smallest one I took into the shelter climbed in and tried to float up and down imagining that I was on one of Campbell's Boats.

Many of the buses had blast netting on the windows. Regular travellers working in Bristol got a special pass to give them priority to get on a bus at the busiest times. The daughter in the cottage next door had one. This was fine if you were travelling the whole distance but unless you got on at the start it could be full when it reached Wraxall.

Dad had a large garden and grew all the vegetables we needed; and more beside. He would give away the spare to friends and neighbours. A local greengrocer heard of this and complained to the "Powers that be" because dad did not have a license to sell vegetables. Mother went to the "food office" at Flax Bourton (part of what was until recently Farleigh Hospital and was originally the Bedminster Workhouse) to ask if this was so. It was confirmed that one must have a license and did she require one? She asked first how much it would cost and was told that they were free. So she obtained the license and dad continued giving away spare vegetables.

Wilfred my brother heard that war had been declared on a train travelling from Birmingham to Bristol. It was loaded with troops going to Avonmouth. Some had come from Scotland and no refreshments were provided throughout the whole journey. The Sergeant Major would get out at each station to see if any food or drink was available. At Gloucester he was only out for a few seconds and jumped back in to tell them war had been declared.

PLACES AND PEOPLE

WRAXALL IN THE WAR YEARS
by Phyllis Horman

Battle Axes	*Mr and Mrs Hall*
The Croft	*Miss Penny*
Court Farm	*Mr and Mrs J Mitchell*
Forge	*Mr Warry*
Gable Farm	*Mr Davies (?)*
Garage	*Mr Neate*
Ham Farm	*Mr Marshall*
Hazel Farm	*The Ball family*
Police	*P.C. Duck*
Post Office	*Mrs M A Ball*
Quarry Farm	*Miss Child*
Rectory	*Mr Briggs*
Rock Farm	*Mr and Mrs P Vowles*
St John (cottage)	*Mr R Coate*
Shoe Shop	*Mr R Mitchell*
Tyntesfield	*Lady Wraxall*
Undertaker	*Mr F Stevens (?)*
Watercress Farm	*Mr and Mrs R Vowles*
Wraxall Court	*(Mr T R Davey died in June 1939)*
" "	*(Mrs T R Davey died there in 1942)*
" "	*(Later Convalescent home for R.N.)*
Wraxall House	*Admiral Sir Hugh and Lady Tweedie*

74th GENERAL HOSPITAL   APO 508
CHRISTMAS CELEBRATIONS

Freda Vowles has been kind enough to provide a programme giving details of "Protestant Christmas Services for 24th December 1944" at what we often refer to as Tyntesfield Hospital. It seems appropriate after listing the names of many of the local people to list here just some of those who had come from the U.S.A. to provide comfort for their wounded colleagues.

Copy of "Protestant Christmas Services" provided by Freda Vowles

THE CHAPEL CHOIR

The Chapel Choir was organised at Hoylake in March, 1944. It has been directed since its organisation by Sgt. Frederick W. Ross, and Lt. Elizabeth Clarke has served as organist and pianist from the beginning. The Chapel Choir now ranks as one of the best in the ETO and it has been a major factor in the success of the Chapel services of the 74th General Hospital. Members participating in the program on Christmas Eve are:

DIRECTOR — Sgt. Frederick W. Ross
ACCOMPANIST — Lt. Elizabeth Clarke

THE CHOIR

Sopranos
- Lt. Mary Eakle
- Lt. Mildred Yoxall
- Lt. Bernice Easley
- Miss Ruth Vowels
- Lt. Dorothy Sidner
- Lt. Elizabeth Hurt
- Lt. Catharine McNiven
- Mrs. Kathleen Gurner

Altos
- Lt. Mary Yeager
- Lt. Betty Kleckner
- Lt. Elizabeth Heffner

Tenors
- Cpl. Robert Daniel
- Cpl. Farrel Norman
- Sgt. Wilford Epling
- Pfc. John Gries

Basses
- Lt. D. D. Hesselgesser
- M Sgt. Lloyd Taylor
- Pfc. Noel Hill
- Cpl. David Choate
- Sgt. T. C. Parker
- Pfc. Clair Sykes

ENGLAND — 74TH GENERAL HOSPITAL — APO

Protestant Christmas Services

CHAPLAIN MICHAEL C. ELLIOTT

Choir Director
—Sgt. Frederick Ross
Pianist
—Lt. Elizabeth Clarke
Chaplain's Ass't
—Cpl. Robert Daniel
Christian Service Club
—M Sgt. Lloyd Taylor

"Glory to God in the highest, and on earth peace, good will towards men."

24th December 1944

ORDER OF SERVICE
10:00 A.M.

Prelude

Call to Worship — Silent Meditation

Invocation — Lord's Prayer in Unison

Choral Amen

Hymn — No. 50 "Holy, Holy, Holy"

Responsive Reading — No. 39

Hymn — No. 53 "O Come All Ye Faithful"

Duet — "Away In A Manger"
 —Sgt. Frederick W. Ross
 —Cpl. Robert R. Daniel

Scripture Reading and Prayer

Offering for Mueller Orphanage

Anthem — "Bethlehem" — Bowker
 —The Chapel Choir

Sermon — A STAR AT MIDNIGHT
 —Chaplain Michael C. Elliott

Benediction

Postlude

CHRISTMAS EVE MUSICAL
8:00 P.M.

Processional — "O Come All Ye Faithful"
Invocation and Choral Amen
Hymn No. 54 "O Little Town of Bethlehem"
Choir — "Gloria In Excelsis"
 "Behold I Bring You Good Tidings"
  —Edwyn A. Clare
Solo — "He Shall Feed His Flock" — Handel
 —Cpl. Robert R. Daniel
Choir — "The Birthday of A King" — Neidlinger
Reading of the Scripture
Prayer
Duet — "Cantique De Noel" — Adams
 —Sgt. Frederick W. Ross
 —Cpl. Robert R. Daniel
Hymn No. 53 "Hark The Herald Angels Sing"
Solo — "Ave Maria" — Schubert
 —Sgt. Frederick W. Ross
Choir — "Bethlehem" — Bowker

Offering for Mueller Orphanage

Choir — "Good King Wenceslas"
 Solos —Sgt. Frederick W. Ross
  —Pfc. Noel Hill
Choir — "The First Christmas" — J. Barnby
 (a) "The Annunciation"
 (b) "The Message to the Shepherds"
 (c) "Cradle Song of the Blessed Virgin"
 (d) "Gloria In Excelsis"
Hymn No. 52 "Joy To The World"
Choir — "Silent Night"
Benediction

CHAPTER TWO
WARTIME MEMORIES - EVACUEES

BACKWELL AND WEST TOWN

PUPILS FROM NORTH HAMMERSMITH CENTRAL MIXED SCHOOL

EVACUATION FROM LONDON TO THE COUNTRY SEPT 1939

by Eileen Hanlon

As an 11 year old I started attending North Hammersmith Central Mixed School in 1938. The fear of war was with us during that year until Neville Chamberlain returned from Germany to Croydon announcing "Peace for our time". I seem to remember that air raid shelters were being dug on Shepherds Bush Green in 1938.

At the new school, we were following with interest in the Geography lesson the travels of the King and Queen who were in Canada and we were learning about that country.

When we broke up for the summer holidays in 1939, we were not to know then that we would never sit at those desks again. We locked our desks as usual and left all our things in them. I left a Bible in my desk which had belonged to my grandfather which had his name and a date in the 1860s in it. My mother was later very sad about this. I had turned 12 by this time and I was not to know that there would definitely be a war. By the time it was all over I would have turned 18 and been at work for four years. I would have experienced being homeless because of the bombing, and doing "Julius Caesar" in the school air raid shelters by the Liverpool docks where I heard from girls of their fathers and brothers being lost in the Navy.

For a week preceding the commencement of the War, we were instructed to attend our school each morning and wait in the playground. Our parents had been instructed to purchase a large rucksack, together with a bakelite cup etc and a small purse.

We had previously had to go with our families to a neighbouring school to be issued with gas masks; later on we had to go back to have another piece fitted on to the end of the gas mask. This was to cope with another type of gas expected; babies and young children were issued with different types of gas masks.

Each day during that week we attended school expecting to go away, only to be told that we would not be going that day and to come back the next.

We stood around in the playground waiting for instructions, excitedly discussing which country would be "on our side" in this war, and feeling apprehensive. The general consensus of opinion of the parents was that it would be "over by Christmas". Some of the mothers were coming with us as helpers.

Finally on Saturday the 2nd September 1939 we were told that this was "it". War was expected and we were off. We walked crocodile fashion along the Uxbridge Road to the Metropolitan Station and got on the train without knowing where we were going. We went to Paddington Station and got on a train still not knowing where we were going. During the journey we were issued with some food in a small brown paper carrier bag with string handles (all I can remember about the food was the bar of chocolate!).

We alighted at Weston-Super-Mare. It was a beautiful day and the sand looked lovely. I remember thinking that it would be nice to be staying there. However we were transferred to coaches and were taken to the Village Hall at West Town. There we waited for people to come and take us home. We were allocated to people according to how many they could take into their home. I was billeted with a family with two other girls, in Station Road, but after some time moved on: the lady could not keep us as she had some relatives of her own coming from London to stay.

We had been instructed to meet on the Sunday at the Cross-roads in West Town at 12 Noon. By then Mr Chamberlain had announced that we were at war with Germany. I remember that the women helpers were all weeping.

I was eventually billeted with Mr & Mrs Powles and their daughter Monica who was a year older than me. They were very kind and treated me the same as Monica and took me everywhere with them.

At first the Junior School, (I was in "Hammersmith juniors") did lessons in a sort of hut in the local recreation ground. The weather was beautiful. Later on, we were allowed to use the badminton hall of the local big house at the end of the village. Every day a barrel of apples would be placed outside the hut and we were told to help ourselves on the way out.

The house was occupied by a Mr and Mrs Robinson. They must have been very public spirited people because Mr Robinson used to set little competitions for us. I remember one was learning the towns of the West Country.

The senior part of the school did their lessons in the badminton hall in the next village of Backwell, which I understood also belonged to a member of the Robinson family.

My recollections of that autumn are of a lovely village with beautifully warm, sunny weather and going for nice walks up on the hills, and an abundance of apples. There was a feeling of apprehension about our parents at home, especially when we heard that an air-raid siren had sounded right after war was declared. It was altogether a strange experience, the villagers coped with the blackout and the need to cover windows in black and masking the headlights of their cars. I think food was probably beginning to be in short supply. I can remember hearing about the "Battle of the River Plate" and the loss of our ships as the winter wore on.

For the Christmas of 1939 Mr and Mrs Powles took me away with them and Monica to Wells in Somerset. We stayed in a lovely rambling house near Wells Cathedral. The winter was a particularly hard one and on the way back to West Town after Christmas I looked out of the back window of the car and all the telegraph poles were askew and heavy with ice. When I got back to school I won the prize for the best essay on how we had spent our first Christmas away from home and how we had felt.

I don't remember doing very much in the way of schooling during this period - although I remember we were reading the book "Dotheboys Hall" from Dickens "Nicholas Nickleby" and we did a lot of knitting - a lot of gloves etc for the Forces - and sewing.

We were taken into Mr Robinson's grounds to learn archery; also the Senior School used to come to West Town for this.

I came home for the Easter of 1940 and, as my father, who was by that time, in the Army (Intelligence Corps or "Field Security Police") was expecting to be posted to an airport or docks in the North of England I did not go back to West Town. Later on in the Autumn we moved to Lancashire where we had moved from two or three years before the war.

In the meantime I could not get back into my school in Hammersmith because the firemen had occupied it but I was allowed to attend another school for the mornings one week and the afternoons the next, then I had to leave there because the firemen needed that school.

Everything seemed very strange to me at home. A brick air raid shelter had been built in the back garden (where later on in the year we spent night after night, all night, during the "Battle of Britain"). All the windows had brown sticky paper on them to prevent flying glass and the park where I played before the war was now all dug up for allotments. When I went up North I found that I was way behind the other girls in French, Maths, etc - our schooling must really have suffered during the first year of the war.

We moved back to London later in the war and were bombed out as our house backed on to houses that were demolished in Godolphin Road Shepherds Bush in 1944. A block of flats now stands there.

I shall always feel involved with the village in Somerset because I met my husband to be there on the Sunday morning that war broke out. He had come away with his sister as the Government policy was to try to keep families together, but after about six weeks he joined his own school which had been evacuated to Guildford. (Wandsworth Technical Institute).

My National Health Number on my medical card is the old Identity Card Number which was issued to me while I was evacuated, so my number is the West Town Code and the "4" means that I was the fourth in the Powles' household. After the war these identity card numbers were used for the medical cards.

I also have happy memories of going tobogganing in the hills at the back of the village, of going into Bristol ice skating with Monica and her friends, of her parents taking us to some nice places in Somerset and into Bristol. At one time we went to listen to Henry Hall playing at the Colston Hall and I remember a three piece ladies orchestra at a little tea place in Park Street I believe.

My husband reminds me that the Ready family used to run a boys club for evacuees; he used to go there to play table tennis.

The corner shop at the junction of the main road and Station Road was used as a clinic for the evacuees and it was a Doctor Jackson who looked after them. I also remember seeing him in a play where he took the part of a solicitor. Dr Jackson lived in the main road and had some of the teachers from our school billeted on him.

LATE FOR SCHOOL!
by Joan Roberts

I joined North Hammersmith Central Mixed School in September 1938. At the outbreak of war my father who had spent 25 years in the Royal Navy expected an immediate recall. My mother attempted to keep the family together and took us three children to Hertfordshire. After a fortnight she realised that the village school would not provide the education she wanted for my sister and I so she arranged for us to catch up with our schools that had been evacuated to separate locations.

My mother brought me by train from London in October 1939 and we went to the billeting officer's home in the Main road. I was taken to Mr and Mrs Cliff whose house was on the main road in West Town. They had to move to Bristol soon after so I was only able to stay there for three months.

District Nurse (Backwell & West Town) Mrs Radford, Terry Radford, Joan Godfrey (now Roberts)

LCC Tag *Joan Roberts*

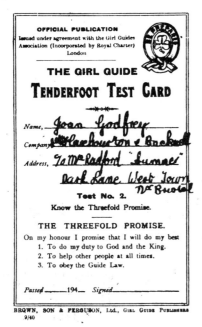

Girl guide Tenderfoot Card
Joan Roberts

In January 1940 I moved in with Olive and Sydney Radford in "Sumner" Dark Lane Backwell where I stayed for three years until I left school. The district nurse also lived with us for about two years.

I remember that an American camp was set up at the end of West Town (*Ed. presumably at Brockley*). It was mostly coloured troops from the Pioneer Corps that dug the ditches and put in the toilets. When they had completed their work the white troops finished off the site.

The school had part of a field on the northern side of the main road. A lot of vegetables that we grew were used by us to make soup on the boiler which heated the badminton hall.

I was able to tour the area with my friend as my parents had bought me a bicycle. Among other memories are being in the Girl Guides; collecting waste paper; a person calling weekly selling savings stamps.

For pocket money I picked cider apples and collected rose hips when in season. I also helped with the harvest but that was voluntary.

I kept in touch with the Radfords but after Olive died about 1985 Sydney went to live with Margaret and Terry in Canada. When Sydney died Terry contacted me and sent some items he thought would interest me. Among them were my ration book and a "tag" that was used to identify evacuees. However the "tag" was not mine. WHO WAS THE PETER EYLES it belonged to and when did he come to Backwell?

(Editor - Does anyone know more about Peter Eyles?)

A HAPPY TIME!
by Grace Golding

I was amused to read Joyce Coyle's recall of changing her wellington boots at Rideout's cottage on Backwell Hill.

(See "Villages at War")

I lived there for 9 months with Mr and Mrs Rideout and another girl Joyce Hill. Mr Rideout was killed in the blackout about Easter 1940, he worked at the railyards in Bristol.

When I left Mrs Rideout I went to Mr and Mrs Ware at Hillview House Farleigh. This was on the main road. I stayed there until I returned to London at the end of 1941. I lost touch after I went to Australia in 1952. The time I was at Backwell was very happy and, but for the war, I might never have had those experiences. I recall vividly as others have the big raid on Filton aerodrome. It seems most of us mistook the enemy planes for friendly ones.

In an earlier letter Grace said:

There was a Home Guard in Backwell. At first only armbands bearing the letters LDV were available. (The volunteers were nicknamed rather unfairly the Look Duck and Vanish brigade). Weapons were scarce at first and any suitable implement was carried. This was later exchanged for a rifle and Army battledress uniform.

Fire watching duties were also carried out by those who were old enough. I don't recall any serious incidents in the village. One enthusiastic watcher was soundly rebuked for going on duty with a saucepan on her head in lieu of a helmet.

COUNTRY MEMORIES
by Stella Harbert

The school had an allotment off the main road between West Town and Farleigh where we were taught to "Dig for Victory". I would also dig up horse radish roots from a lane nearby.

Backwell Girl Guides *Stella Harbert*

Backwell Girl Guides *Stella Harbert*

We picked apples for cider at Williams Cider works at Backwell Common and I remember helping ourselves to bright yellow quinces which we mistook for ripe pears.

On a different note the Parish hall was I remember used as a first aid post. I remember that someone lost the top of their finger and was treated there.

NAILSEA

WORNINGTON ROAD L.C.C. SCHOOL

EVACUATED TO NAILSEA
by Ron Howcroft

I had been at the school from the age of 5 and would have been still in the infants when I came to Nailsea.

After leaving the Royal Oak on arrival in Nailsea I lived with Miss Nora and Miss Muriel Mellick at Springfield, Bucklands Batch for the duration of the war. My brother Jack was with me for a while but then lived elsewhere. He worked on a farm which he believes was East End Farm on the Tickenham / Clevedon border.

Jack, Ron and Rose Howcroft outside Springfields, Bucklands Batch 1940

He lived, not at the farm, but with a family called Izzard. He believes that the farmer was George Arney.

(Editor's Note - George Arney was at that time farming East End Farm which was on the border of Tickenham and Clevedon.

The Arney family came to East End Farm in the 1820's and at least three generations farmed it until George retired in 1972. George married Iris Rose Durbin of Coombe Farm, West End Nailsea who was the sister of Jack Durbin whose memories are related above in Chapter One.

Ron Howcroft who now lives in Fulham went in later years to see his daughter's teacher in London and was surprised to discover that she had been one of the teachers evacuated to Nailsea with him).

TICKENHAM
WE'LL NEVER FORGET
by Gladys Wood

Though we'll never forget our days of being evacuees, there are a number of things we've forgotten especially names of people. But we have put a few memories down.

I had just turned 9 in August, 1939 and my sister was 11yrs 9mths when we were sent away to the country for safety. We caught a train from Paddington carrying our gas masks, going to what we thought was a holiday. Little did we dream it would be for more than 5 years.

Gladys & Margaret with a grandson of the Durbins. *Miss E. Weekes.*

We arrived at Weston super Mare where we were put on coaches and taken to Tickenham Hall. On the way there children were dropped off at different points. When we arrived at the hall, our names ages etc were taken and then we had a carrier bag given to us, though what it contained we cannot remember except for a lovely bar of chocolate.

On the journey to Tickenham we couldn't get over the sight of all the fields and animals, we'd never seen such sights before.

We were allocated to a Mr and Mrs Durbin and when driven to this lovely bungalow with beautiful gardens we were very overawed. Mr Durbin (Pa) greeted us and I remember being frightened of this strange man, and hid behind my sister. We gradually settled in, Mr and Mrs Durbin and Miss Weekes who was a companion and housekeeper to them must have put up with a lot from us. Country life amazed us and like the old jokes we couldn't get over the milk being brought round in a churn and not bottles.

There were a couple of other evacuees whose names we can't remember, though they only stayed for a short time. We went scrumping as we thought the apples on the trees were there for our taking. We got a ticking off and for a while we weren't liked by a few locals.

We attended the local village school, my sister only for a short time before she moved to the senior school at Clevedon. I enjoyed it, especially the sunny lunch times when we were allowed to paddle in the stream. We made friends with the farmers' children and we spent happy days with them and loved to help with haymaking and cornstacking.

You cannot imagine how our lives changed during the time we were away from our parents. We came from a small grocery shop with a back yard and a tin tub for a bath to a lovely home with a proper bathroom, beautiful gardens and the most beautiful scenery that you could wish for.

Even though we were away from the main bombing we used to hear Bristol getting bombed. One day a parachutist came floating down who we believed to be a German. We used to do a lot of cycling with Pa and Dolly as we called them and we always enjoyed that. Miss Weekes (Dolly) used to take us to see her parents at Failand and it was here we saw our first Germans who were POWs. Mr and Mrs Weekes used to have two visit them and one said I reminded him of his daughter. One day when we visited Mr and Mrs Weekes he gave me a ship in a bottle with my name on the ship. It was a lovely surprise and today it has still got pride of place with me.

There were also Italian POWs somewhere near Tickenham who we used to see when cycling home from school. We had some lovely times and happy memories that will always stay with us.

We both left school at 14, my sister worked for a grocery firm in Clevedon which she really enjoyed and the owner thought a lot of her and was sorry to lose her when we came home.

I started work in a shoe shop but it was only for about a year before we left the country for our town life again. There weren't many evacuees who stayed the length of time we did and we'll always be very grateful to our "second" family for teaching us so many things, not least an appreciation of country life which we've always kept.

Footnote - The Farmer who used to come with the milk deliveries was called Mr Shipp. The children were Mr Fords. Our headmaster was Mr Philips. Margaret worked for Mr Sibley. I worked for Lennards.

WRAXALL

From "WRAXALL IN WARTIME"
by Phyllis Horman

When the evacuees came from London we had a little Jewish girl of eight years billeted with us for a while. I was a bit jealous at first as mother and dad tried to make up for the absence of her parents. Later on when the air-raids on Bristol became so bad we had a mother and her son Peter who was about my own age. They would come to us to spend the night often in our air raid shelter and go back home to Raleigh Road Bedminster for the day. Peter suffered from asthma and the worry of the raids made him worse. He was a happy mischievous, good natured lad, and we all liked him very much.

CHAPTER THREE

AIR RAIDS
LOCAL MEMORIES - Extracts from VILLAGES AT WAR

Backwell -

"It was deadly quiet; it was also pitch black because the bomb had cut off the electricity supply. After a while we saw the flickering of torches and called out. The wardens told us to stay where we were because it was unsafe" (VAW)

Nailsea -

"Uncle Sam had a house in Moorfields Lane (now Fosse Lane) the bomb blew doors and windows out and some tiles off the roof. The family .... found the handles of the cups still hanging on the dresser" (VAW)

Tickenham -

"While he was doing that the bull pushed the flaming straw and a bomb into the yard at the front. His eyes were blazing ... (VAW)

Wraxall -

In Wraxall that night a bomb fell about 70 yards north of the Rectory. The Bomb Disposal Squad were apparently satisfied .... (but when it was removed 6 months later it was found to be a 1400 kg UXB!) (VAW)

THE FILTON RAID
25th Sept. 1940

"We thought it was the invasion as we saw some bale out of the planes flying up the valley" (VAW)

Robin Haworth saw the aircraft turn towards Bristol, Eric McEwen Smith thought the planes were British. He found he was wrong when the AA gun at Markham opened up (VAW)

ONE OF THEIR AIRCRAFT FAILED TO RETURN
From information supplied by John Penny

He 111P, Wnr 2126, G1+DN of 5/KG55 was shot down by A.A. fire from Portbury gunsite (237 Battery, 76th HAA Rgt). The aircraft was abandoned by its crew and crashed at Racecourse Farm Failand near Bristol at 11.50 hours. Its crew escaped almost without injury.

They were:-

Oblt	Gottfried Weigel	(F)	P.O.W.
Ofw	Alfred Narres	(B)	P.O.W.
Uffz	Karl Gerdsmeier	(Bm)	P.O.W.
Gefr	Karl Geib	(Bs)	P.O.W.
Fw	Georg Engel	(Bf)	P.O.W. *

* injured taken to Clevedon Cottage Hospital

The Luftwaffe report stated

"Near Bristol there was strong well laid flak. Some shell bursts encountered at a height of 5000m left broad smoke trails suspended in the air.

Although subject to photographic confirmation, it is justifiable from visual observations to think that extensive interference has been caused to production all over the engine factory".

German News Agency reports stated

Formations of the German Air Force bombed the aero engine works at Filton near Bristol this morning. The attack was made in several waves and the bombers which were escorted by fighters scored direct hits on the works. Several air combats ensued but the exact number of enemy aircraft shot down has not been ascertained. The last squadrons of our aircraft were able to assess devastation caused by our bombs. As they left there were thick clouds of smoke over the factory. This factory will not produce many more aircraft.

THE PARACHUTIST
by Phyllis Horman

In a lonely spot across a field on the Wraxall Portbury boundary lived an Aunt and Uncle. Aunt was in the cottage by herself when a German airman parachuted from his damaged aeroplane. She was petrified when he landed in the field in front of the cottage, thinking he was probably armed, yet she went out towards him. She said afterwards that in a minute or two he was surrounded by "enough people to have eaten him".

She was very fond of children and said he looked so young he could have been one of her own boys. I understand she gave him a cup of tea.

(Editor's note - Don Irish mentions in "The Missing Machine Gun" the enterprise exhibited in gaining access to the wreckage; Phyllis heard of another lad who charged people 6d to visit the site.)

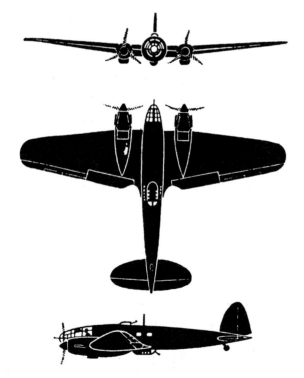

Heinkel 111

THE MISSING MACHINE GUN - A MYSTERY SOLVED?

*by Peter Wright
from a discussion with Don Irish*

(Editors Note As this book was about to go to printers I was told that there was a written report that a machine gun had gone missing from the wreckage of the He 111 at Racecourse Farm. I have so far been unable to verify it but if the rumour is true the mystery is solved!)

At the time of the raid I roamed around with a group of teenage evacuees. The only names I can remember are the Giles Brothers.

We were some of the many who went to see the wreckage at Failand but being more "enterprising" than most managed to gain access to the wreckage probably by distracting the guard at the gate.

We found a machine gun and decided to see how it worked. We wrapped it in sacking and had no trouble in taking it away on our bikes to Bourton Combe where there was a quarry. We had had the luck also to find some ammunition with it.

When we got it there we decided to test it but realised we would have to mount it on something. As there was a gate nearby we tied it to the gate with rope and then pulled the trigger. The gun nearly tore itself from the makeshift mounting and sprayed everything in front with bullets. Fortunately none of us was hurt but we were certainly frightened. It made a hell of a racket.

We disposed of this lethal weapon by burying it and as far as I know it is still there buried many feet below the surface.

RAIDS ON BACKWELL
Compiled by Peter Wright

At the beginning of August 1940 Backwell was honoured by being the recipient of a considerable quantity of waste paper dropped from a German Heinkel 111. At least that is what I believe the local inhabitants thought of the paper they found the next day. It was a leaflet containing a speech by Adolf Hitler. Many copies have survived and one is illustrated earlier. It was provided by John Brain.

Maureen Chlupac sent me a photocopy of part of the leaflet several years ago when she wrote from Australia. She told me that when a later raid took place she remembers that her father, who was a warden, had just come into the house when the blast of a bomb blew him down the hall. Their house was quite severely damaged on both 4th and 11th April 1941.

Details of the Leaflet raid are contained in Appendix 4.

On 16th March Isabel Robinson recorded a raid that lasted from 21.15hrs to 04.00hrs the next morning. This was the occasion of a major raid on Bristol. About 150 HEs dropped in Brockley Woods.

It was about this time that Mr Greenhill in Nailsea was asking that a siren be placed in Nailsea despite previous requests of the Parish Council being turned down.

Backwell experienced very heavy raids on the 4th and 11th of April 1941. Damage was done to Oldfield House in both raids and in the second raid damage was done to Firgrove and the Gallops and a horse was killed. Despite these close calls nobody was killed.

AIR RAID ON NAILSEA
16/17 JUNE 1941

Eileen Derry was under the stairs; she heard the plane coming and then the sound of bombs....... (VAW)

Len Price emerged from the damaged cottage knowing the Austins had been injured. With Eileen he ran up the lane to get Dr Gornall.....

One bomb hit a pair of cottages at Nowhere killing Mr Austin and seriously injuring his wife.

Another bomb destroyed one of a pair of bungalows in Station Road near to the (new) junction with Queens Road. The Thorburn family who lived there were in their Anderson shelter and were unhurt as were the two ladies living in the adjoining bungalow who I understand were unaware of their near miss until the next day.

Mrs Austin spent nearly eighteen months in hospital with her injuries. (For further details see "Villages at War")

In his letter which accompanied the details given below and in the Appendix John Penny says

"Looking at Nailsea's fatal incident I thought you might like to have the details

Nowhere - The Derry Family and Mrs Austin (extreme right) shortly before the raid.

The German view of Nailsea

from the German side, especially as the two reports match up so perfectly, something that does not always happen! As you will see they agree on time, both say 01.35 hours: and they agree on number and size of bombs with the Germans saying 16 of the SC50 (50kg general purpose bombs) and the British also counting sixteen 50kg bombs (15 exploded and 1UXB).

On the day of their attack they had just moved from their old base at Vannes in Brittany to Chartres south of Paris. As the report says they lost half of their force to nightfighters and one aircraft deposited half of its load on what it thought was Bristol. This aircraft reported to have bombed Bristol "visually" and this was probably due to British electronic counter-measures which were in use at the time and were known to have caused interference to the German X-beams making Hucclecote difficult to locate. *(see Appendix 2)*

The aircraft probably mistook the Downside "Starfish" decoy site at ST 477661 for Bristol just as the British intended and the sad result was the death of a villager.

The full details of the Luftwaffe Report appear in Appendix No 5 the details given below relate only to the bombing of Nailsea.

CIVIL DEFENCE REPORT

The Civil Defence Report for the period from 06.00 hrs Monday June 16th 1941 to 06.00 hrs Tuesday June 17th 1941 has the following entry

SOMERSET Long Ashton R.D. Nailsea
01.35 Hrs, 15 HEs (50kg) and 1 UXB were dropped in a line running NE to SW over a distance of about a mile near Station Road between the east end of Nailsea and the GWR. ....

LUFTWAFFE REPORT
Night Operations 16/17 June 1941.
BRISTOL
KGr 100 operating 1 He 111 based at Vannes attacked Bristol as an alternative to the Gloster Aeroplane Factory at Hucclecote. It reached the target at 01-35 hours andattacked it from 3400 metres bombing visually with 16 SC 50.

———————————

(Editor - In "Villages at War" the impression was given that the German aircraft had jettisoned its bomb load in an endeavour to escape ack ack fire and searchlights. It now seems that that impression was wrong. The attack seems to have been deliberate but misdirected.

CHAPTER FOUR

1946 THE END OR THE BEGINNING?

A PRISONER RETURNS HOME
by Helmuth Horst.

(Editor - Helmuth Horst told me when I met him that he liked the British way of life and had been well treated during the time he spent here as a prisoner of war.)

"After the end of hostilities I had been acting as an interpreter on the Isle of Wight where the "German Prisoner of War Working Company" had been repairing a sea wall near Freshwater in conjunction with British firms. In September 1946 I returned to Old Dean Common Camp at Camberley where I received my release documents and was sent with other P.O.W.s to Backwell".

German POW's Old Dean Common Camp, Camberley-Surrey 1946 Helmuth Horst second from right back row.

I must have been at Backwell between 23 and 29th September 1946. I remember Backwell station from where we were taken by lorry to the camp.

The camp must have been outside the village because I have not seen any houses nearby. The camp was rather small with nissen huts. As far as I remember there was a stonewall to the left and to the right side of the gate.

After a week we went by train to Hull where we arrived the same afternoon going straight on board the EMPIRE HALBERD. Next day 1st October 1946 we arrived at Cuxhaven Germany."

His war was over.

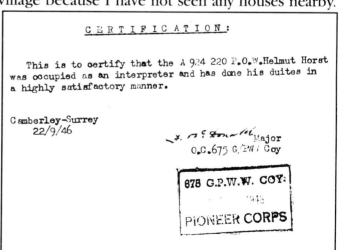

WOULD IT BE "PEACE FOR OUR TIME"?

APPENDIX 1

AMERICAN UNITS NEAR THIS AREA

from information supplied by Ken Wakefield

FIRST US ARMY STATION LIST
Units in the West Country 31st May 1994

    1st Engr Brig Sp
    602nd Engr Cam Bn   Det Tyntesfield, Som.
    602nd Engr Cam Bn (less Co'D') Tyntesfield, Som. (two entries)

    310th Ord Bn
    18th Ord MM Co   Failand, Som

    101st Ord Amm Bn
    624th Ord Amm Co   Failand

    162nd QM Bn M
    554th QM Rlhd Co   Churchill
    14th Cml Maint Co   Brockley, Som
    60th Cml Depot Co   (Flax?) Bourton, Som
    84th Cml Co Sg   Nailsea

ARMY TROOPS

    581st QM Sales Co   Tyntesfield
    23rd Cml Bn Sg   Bristol
    2nd Radio Broad Co M   Tyntesfield
    72nd Pub Sv Bn   Tyntesfield
    92nd Cml Bn Mtz   Brockley

In his letter dated 10th April 1991 Ken Wakefield adds

> "I can only guess at some of the US Army abbreviations but those known to me are as follows : Cam = Camouflage. Bn = Battalion, Det = Detachment, MM = Medium Maintenance, Cml = Chemical, Qm = Quartermaster, Broad = Broadcasting, Sv = Service, Mtz = Motorised".

THE AIRSTRIP AT BEGGARS BUSH LANE

"With regard to your comment in "Villages at War" I can confirm that there was an airstrip at Beggars Bush lane ("Beggar" on the present road sign, but "Beggars" with an "s" on pre war/wartime Ordnance Survey Maps). This airstrip was actually located on the Clifton College sports field and was used by liaison aircraft of HQ First US Army and, later on by HQ Ninth US Army".

APPENDIX 2

TECHNICAL NOTES
from information supplied by John Penny

"LUFTWAFFE REPORT"

"The night attack on the Gloster Aircraft Co at Hucclecote near Gloucester by four aircraft of KGr 100 used X-Verfahren". (See Appendix 5)

2/ 1. Kampfgruppe 100 was the Luftwaffe's specialist pathfinder Gruppe which flew Heinkel He 111's and navigated to their targets along electronic beams (X-Verfahren).

On the day of their attack on Hucclecote they had just moved from their old base at Vannes in Brittany to Chartres south of Paris. As the report below shows they lost half of their force to nightfighters and one aircraft deposited half of its load on what it thought was Bristol.

This aircraft reported to have bombed Bristol "visually" and this was probably due to British electronic countermeasures which were in use at the time and were known to have caused interference to the German X-beams making Hucclecote difficult to locate.

The aircraft probably mistook the Downside "Starfish" decoy site at ST 477661 for Bristol just as the British intended and the sad result was the death of a villager.

2/ 2. X-Verfahren - was a system for navigation and accurate bombing using signals from two widely separated points on the continent near to the coast facing Britain.

2/ 3. Operation of X-Verfahren - one radio beam was laid onto the target from a position on the Cherbourg peninsular. This was used by the attacking aircraft to guide their approach.

For the attack on Hucclecote three cross beams were transmitted from Audembart SW of Calais.

These crossed the approach beam at 50km, 20km and 5km from the target.

When the first cross beam signal was heard on the attacking aircraft it acted as a warning. When the second was heard the observer started his bomb release clock.

When he heard the third he again pressed a button and one hand on the clock stopped and another started. When the two hands overlapped at the previously computed bomb release point the bombs were released automatically.

2/ 4. British Counter Measures

British scientists had anticipated the use by the Germans of devices to enable them to navigate and bomb by beams laid onto the target and were often able to detect the transmissions. By doing so they were often able to calculate which cities were the intended targets and sometimes transmit false signals to mislead the bombers.

Lights and flares were often made visible to simulate a city to decoy the German aircraft and encourage them to drop their bombs in open countryside.

2/ 5. It is interesting to note that while the Luftwaffe seem to have been misled by the Lulsgate "Decoy" in the Good Friday raid described by John Brain the Luftwaffe Report three months earlier for "Night Operations 4/5th January 1941" states:-

Target: Major attack on Avonmouth ..... A very large Decoy Light installation was located west-south-west of Bristol and was made up of white, green, and red lights.

Nearby, burning decoy installations were perceived .....

APPENDIX 3

GERMAN BOMBER FORCES INVOLVED IN THE RAID ON FILTON 25 SEPT. 1940
from information and comments (#) supplied by John Penny

LUFTWAFFE REPORT

Daytime Operations 25 September 1940
Luftflotte 3
Fliegerkorps V
Target: Large scale attack on the Bristol Aeroplane Co. factory at Filton.

Operational Summary

Bombers
- 68   Aircraft despatched to Filton
- 58   Aircraft attacked Filton (inc 1 crashed on return)
- 6   Aircraft aborted due to engine problems
- 4   Aircraft missing

On Filton 87.7 tonnes H.E.
300 SC 250, 26 SC 250 LZZ, 24 Flam 250 and 4 SC 50.

Fighter Escort
- 52   twin engine fighters despatched
- 2   aircraft lost
- 2   aircraft damaged
- 51   single engined fighters despatched, none lost.

St/KG55
operating 5 He 111's based at Villacoublay.
2 He 111's attacked Filton between 11.45 and 11.50 hours with SC 250, hits reported in the western part of the engine factory.

3 He 111's aborted due to engine problems.

I/KG 55
operating 21 He 111's based at Dreux. 2 He 111's attacked Filton at 11.45 hours with 68 SC 250 and 17 SC 250 LZZ. Bombs landed accurately on the western part of the target.

2 He 111's aborted due to engine problems.
1 He 111 lost
He 111P Wnr 6305, G1+BH of 1/KG 55

> (# force-landed at Westfield Farm Studland near Swanage at 12.10hrs after attack by P/O J. S. Wigglesworth Hurricane 238 Sqn (Middle Wallop) and P/O J Curchin Spitfire 609Sqn (Middle Wallop))

II/KG55

operating 24 He 111's based at Chartres. 20 He 111's attacked Filton at 11.40 hours with 150 SC 250 and 24 Flam 250. 15 hits spread over 5 factory buildings. Many hits directly north and south of the large factory complex. The aircraft factory was hit also hits between the factory and test beds were seen. 1 additional hit on the railway track at the rectangular shaped junction nearby.

1 He 111 aborted due to engine trouble
2 He 111's lost
1 He 111 crashed on return to France.

He 111P, Wnr 2126, G1+DN of 5/KG55

Oblt	Gottfried Weigel	(F)	P.O.W.
Ofw	Alfred Narres	(B)	P.O.W.
Uffz	Karl Gerdsmeier	(Bm)	P.O.W.
Gefr	Karl Geib	(Bs)	P.O.W.
Fw	Georg Engel	(Bf)	P.O.W. injured taken to Clevedon Cottage Hospital

(# shot down by A.A. Fire from Portbury gunsite (237 Battery, 76th HAA Rgt). Aircraft abandoned by crew and crashed at Racecourse Farm Failand near Bristol at 11.50 hours.)

He 111P, Wnr 1525, G1+EP of 6/KG 55

(# attacked by F/O I.N. Bayles & Sgt K.C. Holland in Spitfires of 152 Sqn (Warmwell) and P/O J. R. Urwin-Mann & Sgt R Little in Hurricanes of 238 Sqn (Middle Wallop). It crashed at Church Farm Wolverton near Frome, 1 survivor only. Sgt K.C. Holland's Spitfire crashed at Woolverton as a result of return fire. He was killed.)

Norman Searle was that day out in a van near Radstock ... saw a Heinkel hit and some of the crew bale out ... The rear gunner continued to engage the fighter ... which crashed near the German plane. Both gunner and British pilot were killed. (VAW)

He 111P, Wnr 1579, G1+AP of 6/KG55

(# Damaged by fighters in combat over England. Crash landed at Caen, France 50% damaged)

III/KG 55

    operating 18 He 111's based at Villacoublay. 17 He 111's attacked Filton at 11.45 hrs with 74 SC 250 and 24 Flam 250. 10 to 12 hits on the assembly halls in the east part of the aircraft factory, also hits on the railway junction to the west of the target and on the south east corner of the airfield. 1 He 111 lost.

He 111P, Wnr 2803, G1+LR of 7/KG 55

    (# attacked by P/O N le C Agazarian in a Spitfire of 609 Sqn (Middle Wallop) and P/O J. R. Urwin-Mann of 238 Sqn (Middle Wallop). Also engaged by P/O Miller in a Spitfire of 609 Sqn. Crashed on "Chatsworth", Westminster Road, Branksome Park, Poole, Dorset at 12.08 hours. 4 killed 1 P.O.W.).

In the Bristol area an unidentified wedge shaped, single seater fighter with an enclosed radial engine was seen. It was very manoeuverable, but not as fast as the Bf 110's. Over Bristol were 25 Spitfires and Hurricanes, of which one was claimed shot down by an He 111.

Near Bristol there was strong well laid flak. Some shell bursts encountered at a height of 5000m left broad smoke trails suspended in the air.

Although subject to photographic confirmation, it is justifiable from visual observations to think that extensive interference has been caused to production all over the engine factory.

(Editor's Note: Details of fighter escort have been omitted.)

From German News Agency reports

Formations of the German Air Force bombed the aero engine works at Filton near Bristol this morning. The attack was made in several waves and the bombers which were escorted by fighters scored direct hits on the works. Several air combats ensued but the exact number of enemy aircraft shot down has not been ascertained. The last squadrons of our aircraft were able to assess the devastation caused by our bombs. As they left there were thick clouds of smoke over the factory. This factory will not produce many more aircraft.

APPENDIX 4

GERMAN BOMBER FORCES INVOLVED IN THE LEAFLET RAID 1/2 AUG 1940
from information and comments (#) supplied by John Penny

CIVIL DEFENCE REPORT

Backwell

23.59 hours. The first leaflet raid on Britain. An enemy aircraft flying at a considerable height dropped an estimated several thousand leaflets over the locality. The aircraft was heard circling around for half an hour, apparently without doing anything, before dropping the leaflets which were contained in brown paper bundles. These were secured by a simple wire device which was broken open by a small explosive charge, thereby opening the bundle some distance from the ground and allowing individual leaflets to fall out.

Some people reported a kind of popping noise in the sky no doubt caused when the parcels burst open. The leaflets themselves contained four 18" x 12" pages, each printed in three columns on one folded sheet and headlined "A Last Appeal To Reason".......

LUFTWAFFE REPORT

NIGHT OPERATIONS 1/2 August 1940

LUFTLOTTE 3

Fliegerkorps V

TARGETS: Leaflet raids on the Bristol and Southampton areas.

II/KG 55

Operating 4 He 111s based at Chartres took off at 21.30 hrs

2 He 111's with 14 packs of leaflets dropped over Southampton

2 He 111's with 14 packs of leaflets dropped over Bristol

The same night a further 2 He 111's of II/KG 55 took off at 22.00 hrs from Chartres with Aircraft factories at Filton and Yate as the principal targets and the storage tanks at Avonmouth as an alternative. Neither found these targets; one attacked "a factory near Bristol" and the other a searchlight installation near Bristol.

APPENDIX 5

GERMAN BOMBER FORCES INVOLVED IN THE RAID 16/17 JUNE 1941

from information and comments (#) supplied by John Penny

LUFTWAFFE REPORT

Night Operations 16/17 June 1941

Luftflotte 3

Fliegerkorps IX

Target: Attack on the Gloster Aircraft Co. at Hucclecote near Gloucester by four aircraft of KGr 100 using X-Verfahren

The planned route to the target was from a Radio Beacon near Vannes to Alderney and then to join the Cherbourg main approach X-beam in mid channel. From there the beam which was laid on a bearing of 351 degrees (T) led to the target. The cross beams originated from the Wotan I transmitter at Audembert immediately SW of Calais.

Bombing was carried out between 01.06 and 01.20 hrs from 3400 to 5600 metres with 48 SC50 and 32 SD 50. The return track was direct to the Paimpol Radio Beacon and thence to the beacon near Vannes airfield. One aircraft attacked Bristol as an alternative target. Two aircraft failed to return.

He 111H-2 Wnr 5462, 6N+CH of 1/KGr 100

Uffz.	Franz Koster	(B)	Killed
Oberfw.	Heinz Ittner	(F)	Killed
Gefr.	Wolfgang Porada	(Bf)	Killed
Gefr.	Heinz Keul	(Bs)	Killed
Uffz.	Heinz Berwig	(Bm)	Killed

\# Shot down en-route to Hucclecote by P/O W. M. Gosland and Sgt. Phillips in Beaufighter R2085 of 604 Sq.(Middle Wallop). Crashed 01-20 hours at Home Farm, Maiden Bradley, Wilts. The body of Uffz. Berwig was not discovered until 11 March 1944 and subsequently buried at Haycombe Cemetery, Bath.

He 111H-3, Wnr 5633, 6N+CL of 3/KGr 100

Fw.	Georg Deininger	(F)	P.O.W.
Oblt.	Heinz Pohner	(B)	Killed
Fw.	Kurt Ott	(Bf)	Killed
Fw.	Otto Hertzberg	(Bs)	Killed
Fw.	Karl Engels	(Bm)	Killed

\# Shot down on return from Hucclecote by F/Lt D. S. Pain AFC and F/O Davies in a Beaufighter of 68 Sq (High Ercall). Crashed at 01.50 hours on Combe Hill, Bratton, Wilts.

BRISTOL

KGr 100 operating 1 He 111 based at Vannes attacked Bristol as an alternative target at 01-35 hours from 3400 metres bombing visually with 16 SC 50.

THE CIVIL DEFENCE REPORT
for the period from 06.00 hrs Monday June 16th 1941 to 06.00 hrs Tuesday June 17th 1941 has the following entry

SOMERSET Long Ashton R.D. Nailsea

01.35 Hrs, 15 HEs (50kg) and 1 UXB were dropped in a line running NE to SW over a distance of about a mile near Station Road between the east end of Nailsea and the GWR. The H.E.s started 270 yards south of the Kennels, to 200 yards ENE of "Coombe Grange" and 550 yards NW of Nailsea Station. "Hillcrest" a bungalow in Station Road was demolished and "Showhouse" a cottage at Nowhere Lodge Lane was seriously damaged (1 killed, 1 injured). 5 cows were killed, 3 injured including one later destroyed, while the UXB fell in a field called Long Ground near Marshall's Farm, 400 yards NW of Brook Farm, in the corner of the field by the river.

Casualties: 1 killed, 2 slightly injured.

CASUALTY LIST (FATALITIES)

16/17 June 1941

SOMERSET

LONG ASHTON R.D.

At East End Cottages Nailsea

AUSTIN, Sidney (69) Husband of Alice Emily Austin

APPENDIX 6

CONTRIBUTORS, SOURCES, BIBLIOGRAPHY.

John Brain -

A lifetime resident of Backwell, chorister and bellringer at St Andrew's Parish Church, Backwell; editor of the Parish magazine and son of the Village Baker.

Ella Brake -

Farmer's widow, lived at Battens farm during the war and now lives at Yatton.

Maureen Chlupac -

Lived in West Town during the war, emigrated to Australia.

Muriel Chorley -

Daughter of family that operated the Nailsea sub Post Office during the war.

Jack Durbin -

Farmed Coombe Farm West End, with his father during the war and still lives in Nailsea with his wife.

Grace Golding -

An ex-pupil of North Hammersmith Central Mixed School and a friend of Stella Harbert. Now lives in Australia.

Mary Gornall -

Widow of Doctor Gornall who practiced in Nailsea. She now lives in Birmingham but has friends still in the area. She spent some time teaching at the Fairfield School in Backwell which is the subject of the article by Barbara Lambert.

Eileen Hanlon -

A contributor both to this book and Villages at War. She was an evacuee with the North Hammersmith Central Mixed School and retains a fondness for Backwell which is evident from her writing.

Stella Harbert -

Now lives in Essex and contributed to Villages at War as an ex pupil of North Hammersmith Central Mixed School that was evacuated to Backwell.

Phyllis Horman -

An enthusiastic supporter of N&DLHS and compiler of two books published by the Society. A frequent contributor to Pennant and a lifelong resident of the area. Author of "Wraxall in Wartime" a "Research Paper" published by N&DLHS which forms the basis of her Wraxall memories included here.

Helmuth Horst -

An ex-prisoner of war, now living in Tanneweg, Tubingen, Germany who called on Peter Wright while visiting Weston-super-Mare c1993.

Ron Howcroft -

The only ex-pupil of Wornington Road School that has so far been contacted. He still retains an interest in the area.

Don Irish -

Lived at Flax Bourton during the war and joined the Gordon Highlanders in 1945. Soon after being demobbed he went into catering and worked for most of his career at Barrow Hospital. Remembers delivering telegrams to Tyntesfield Hospital and Barrow which was a Royal Navy Hospital during the war. Has lived in Nailsea since 1960.

Cecil Keel -

Son of the licensees of the Butchers Arms. Still lives in Nailsea.

Dora Keel -

Ran the Butchers Arms with her husband from 1935 until his death. She left soon after in 1958 but still lives nearby.

Clifford Kortright -

Farmworker, bellringer, whose memories of wartime have been of critical importance in preparing this volume and its predecessor.

Miss Barbara Lambert -

Started a school in Backwell on September 25th 1935 from which she retired 30 years later.

Nailsea and District Local History Society (N&DLHS) -

The Society was founded about 20 years ago and produces Pennant q.v. Has been closely involved in research into three major sites in Nailsea and has published nearly 50 books and pamphlets. Is currently involved in bringing its publications up to date and producing a number of new ones.

North Hammersmith Central Mixed School -

Bryony Road, Shepherds Bush, London W 12 was evacuated to the villages of West Town and Backwell, Somerset. At the time of its evacuation Mr Jamison was Head Master but by November 1942 his name had been deleted from the school's headed notepaper and Mr R.C. Keates who had come to Nailsea as Head Master of Wornington Road School was signing testimonials.

from BACKWELL LOCAL NOTES   by Isabel A Robinson
a booklet published privately by the author

October 9th 1939   -   Many of those evacuated from Poplar have returned to their homes ... A large school from Hammersmith ... is being taught in the Badminton Houses at West Town and Backwell houses. The Parish Hall and the W.I. Hut are also being used for this purpose.

December 25th 1939 - Our Central School is still with us and all is well organised. Practically all the mothers have returned home.

July 18th 1945 - On this day (Thursday) the Hammersmith Central School left Backwell ....

Pennant -

The Local History Journal of Backwell, Nailsea, Tickenham and Wraxall is produced by N&DLHS about 4 times a year.

John Penny -

Corresponded with Peter Wright following the publication of "Villages at War" and subsequently supplied many details relating to the Luftwaffe Operations unearthed in many years of research.

Author of "Luftwaffe Operations over Bristol 1940/44" recently published by the Bristol Branch of the Historical Association.

Joan Roberts -

Joined North Hammersmith Central Mixed School in September 1938. Evacuated at first to Hertfordshire and then to Backwell.

Villages at War: Backwell Nailsea Tickenham and Wraxall 1939-45

A local history of the war years, over 1500 copies sold.
by Peter Wright ISBN 0 9516257 0 5 Pub 1990 by the author in association with N&DLHS. Price £2-99 (£3-50 by post UK, £4 overseas).

Contains information gathered by the author from approximately 25 recorded interviews and 40 questionnaires.

Quotations from this book identified by "(VAW)"

Ken Wakefield -

Pilot, author, TV script writer.

Corresponded with Peter Wright to provide more information after the publication of "Villages at War". He had provided the aerial photograph of Nailsea taken by the Luftwaffe used in that book but without acknowledgement as its source was unknown. Due acknowledgement is now given for its use both in "Villages at War" and in this volume.

He is the author of three books found both useful and interesting in putting together the memories of those people who spent the war years in the area.

"TARGET FILTON"

The two Luftwaffe attacks in September 1940 Pub 1990
by Redcliffe Press Ltd ISBN 1 872971 55 5

"OPERATION BOLERO" -

The Americans in Bristol and the West Country Pub 1994
by Crecy Books Limited ISBN 0 947554 51 3

For more details regarding the use of the airstrip at Beggars Bush lane and the aircraft used see

"THE FIGHTING GRASSHOPPERS"

pub. by Midland Counties Pubns.

Miss E. M. Weekes -

Lived and worked near Orchard Avenue in Tickenham from 1935 to 1956. Had much to do with looking after two evacuees who were billeted with her employer.

Gladys Wood -

She was evacuated to Tickenham with her sister where they were billeted with Mr and Mrs Durbin and Miss Weekes. Gladys now lives at Clacton on Sea.

Wornington Road L.C.C. School

Sited in North Kensington not far from Wormwood Scrubs. Many children from this school were evacuated to Nailsea. They were accompanied by the headmaster Mr R C Keates and members of staff. It is interesting to note that by November 1942 Mr Keates is signing Testimonials for North Hammersmith Central Mixed School.